Table of Contents

Dedicated to my children:
Stefani and Milan.

Without you there would be no story to tell.

Special THANKS to my friends/editors:

Mr. Howard Schmid
(my 9th grade English teacher)

Linda Adams
Tim Chen
Peter Hambesis
David Mikrut
Gloria Prince
Will Vivo
LaDella Whitaker

THE RESULT

The Secret In Using Current Results
To Achieve Your Ultimate Goals!

(The Rubber Band Story)

Introduction

Do you tell stories to illustrate a point? As a teacher of 18 years I have been known to tell a story or two. The stories are used as a way to explain a concept to the student in a memorable way. The ideas behind the stories are meant to "stick" inside the student's brain in such a way that they are able to quickly reference them in the future.

Do all of the stories you tell have to be true? Well, the story you are about to read is a true story. Heck, I won't even change the names to protect the guilty. It is based on what happened between my children and me during the summer of 2009. There are a few minor modifications in order to make the story more entertaining. However, those changes do not take away from its main message.

Do you retell your stories? I have found myself telling this story in almost every class I have taught since the events occurred. By telling it early in the semester, I find myself referencing it numerous times to illustrate its main message as it applies to a question or a situation in the course.

I started to see that the message is very important and could be of service. I decided that I should capture the lesson in a short story. To the best of my ability, this book is the effort to capture the message. As someone who has read many "Who Moved My Cheese" type of books, I also want it to be easy to read and understand. In addition, I also included a chapter at the end where I show some applications of this story to various situations.

So why invest a few hours that it will take to read this story? Beside the important message and its application in many areas, I believe that most of us are on a journey to improve our lives. Any tool that we acquire along the way may enhance our self worth and well being. A small nugget of useful and applied information can empower our lives forever.

I urge you to take on the challenges and enjoy the journey. When you reach your goal(s), hopefully the results will be worthwhile and rewarding to you. For your journey, I offer this simple tool.

Enjoy!

Robert Trajkovski March 24, 2010

Before the Practice

It was about eight o'clock on a Friday night. My daughter Stefani called me from my ex-wife's house to catch up on the day's events. It had been a hectic day at school and she wanted to talk about it. Being a beautiful seventh grader, an exceptional student, great athlete, and class president meant that she had a lot on her plate.

She told me that everything had gone well. I asked her if any boy had winked at her. She laughed and told me that she would not tell me if he had. We laughed and continued our conversation for a while.

My son Milan, pronounced Me-lan and meaning "dear", and I also spoke about his day. Like Stefani's day, his day was very uneventful and we joked about his favorite class, 5th grade math. Milan told me that he wants to be an Astrophysicist so I explained to him that being great in math is very important for that field.

As we were about to end our conversation, Milan passed the telephone back to my daughter. Stefani told me that her mom had to work tomorrow and asked me if I could take her to her basketball practice.

I agreed and said that I would meet them at 9 o'clock in the morning at their home. Her practice was scheduled to start at 10 a.m. We said our good nights and I love yous.

Next morning I picked up both kids on time at 9 o'clock and we drove to the gym where the practice was to take place. We got there around 9:30. Since we were the first to arrive at practice, Stefani decided to practice her shooting while Milan and I horsed around. Her shots were going in consistently, except those shots from the free-throw line. Her whole team had the same problem with free-throw shots. In past games, it seemed as if toward the end of the game, the whole team struggled and at times choked at the free-throw line.

The team also had another challenge, their attitude about playing the game. They showed up at the gym at about 10 o'clock or later and it was exhausting to just watch them as they came in. Their warm-up looked as if it were being performed in slow motion. Recent games had not gone any better. Typically, they were competitive but when the opposing team put them on the free-throw line, they were very inconsistent. Most often, the poor performance at the free-throw line resulted in a loss.

Milan and I decided not to get in the way of practice any more and we left. My son and I enjoy our time together. He likes being alone with me because he gets to pick 100% of the activities and does not have to negotiate with his big sister.

His choice was to go to the GameStop store. Luckily, there was one nearby. I remember when I first started playing games back in the early eighties. It was very unusual for anyone to get to the end of a game. Amazingly, with the help of cheat codes, he gets through most games quickly and is always asking for a new game. He wanted to see if there were any good deals on used games.

One of Milan's strengths has always been his strategic thinking. There have been many instances when Stefani and I were trying to resolve a problem and although it seemed that he was not paying attention, Milan offered a suggestion that made the most sense.

Let me give you an example. During one of our group "projects", all three of us were at a hardware store debating which color florescent paint to use to paint numbers on a sidewalk. Stefani and I were trying to get into the brains of our potential customers. Milan, on the other hand, was about four feet away from us looking at another portion of the spray paint isle. Both of us got angry with him and told him that he was not contributing to our decision. He looked at us and told us that he was considering using a different type of handle for us to use, instead of just pressing the button on top of the can. Milan thought that this would give us more control when spraying and produce a better final product. It was very hard to argue against his logic.

Milan also has a knack for strategy games. There are a few games on my smart phone which I have played and played and barely got a decent score. Then Milan would play them behind me and put my high scores to shame. But that's Milan. He never seems to have to try very hard to get great results.

During the Practice

After spending considerable time at the game store, and a few other department stores, we decided to head back to the gym. Stefani had already told us that the team was going to take their lunch break from 12:00 to 12:30 and that she wanted us to bring her something to eat. She said it had to be something light, so that she could continue to play.

Since our choices were limited in the area, we decided to go to Subway and take advantage of the $5 deal. I was not hungry. Milan got a foot long so he could split it with his sister. She wanted a six inch veggie-sub and he got a six inch meatball sub. That is typical of how different they are, even in their food choices.

As we returned to the gym, it was time to go back and eat lunch. The team seemed very busy practicing when the coaches called for a half hour lunch break. Everyone spread out across the bleachers to give themselves enough space and started to eat.

Our conversation dealt mostly with Stef's frustration with the team's performance. She wanted her teammates to just get better or at least act like they wanted to get better. I think that at times she wanted that for them more than they wanted it for themselves. Milan and I patiently listened and mostly nodded. At times Milan tried to change the subject but she always brought us back to the topic.

Stefani expressed that she was worried about the team's free throw performance. She could not stop worrying about how it affected their team's win-loss record. I have offered many suggestions to Stefani in the past but it seemed best to be painfully quiet at this time.

The coach called everyone back and the team slowly, because of their full stomachs, started practicing again. I kept thinking how hard it would be for an adult to go back to practice right after lunch with a full stomach.

While the team started their warm-up exercises, I watched for changes in their attitudes about playing the game that were there earlier. They were missing. Maybe lunch fixed those attitudes?

Milan and I were sitting there for a while when he offered a suggestion. "Hey Dad, why don't we go outside and play at the playground? Stefani will be done in about an hour and we can step out for a little bit without missing much of the practice." I disagreed and told him that I wanted to see the rest of the practice.

As we sat there, Milan grew increasingly bored. After asking me for my smart phone and playing the games that are on it, he repeated his request.

"C'mon Dad... let's go outside and play. I am bored. I don't want to watch Stefani practice. I would rather play outside. It is so much nicer to be outside than inside."

Now, the Dad in me was torn. I wanted to be at both places at once. I wanted to watch the game while still playing outside with Milan. What is a Dad to do? How do I manage to be supportive of Stefani and play outside with Milan without upsetting either one?

While I sat wondering and staring into help me land, in front of me was the answer. On the floor laid a rubber band. Fifteen feet to our left was a large, square trash can. A light bulb lit above my head.

I stood up, retrieved the rubber band, and offered the following suggestion. "Milan, from the bench, if you can hit the inside of that trash can with this rubber band I will take you to the playground."

I figured that accomplishing this task could take a while, require a great deal of effort, and that eventually Milan would give up. In the mean time, I would get to enjoy the practice while he would make repeated trips to the can area to retrieve the rubber band and plot his strategy.

Milan looked at the rubber band and said, "You are on." As we sat on the bench he took the rubber band in his hand, aimed his index finger towards the trash can, and let the rubber band rip. "Swoooosh", it went. He let out a sigh; it missed the trash can by a foot, by landing in front of it.

It was back to the drawing board. He concluded that he needed to increase the angle. So he went to the rubber band and picked it up. Eagerly dashing back to the bench, he took another guess at the perfect trajectory needed to hit his target. He carefully aimed and shot the rubber band. But this time the rubber band flew and flew over the trash can and landed about 5 feet behind it.

At this point, I wondered how much that rubber band could be stressed before it broke. Wisely Milan pondered the same problem as he went to pick up the rubber band.

Milan, the strategist, was stumped. He saw the rubber band land in front and behind the can. Maybe the secret was to find the perfect angle that was needed in order to hit his target? However, he had no way of recording the angle that he had used for his last attempt. So, for every shot he had to result to approximations of the previously used angle.

With each attempt at finding the perfect angle, slight adjustments were made, and the rubber band continued to bounce off the can at various spots. Consequently, with each undesirable result, Milan resorted to adjusting what he previously thought was the perfect angle.

After several attempts, he concluded that maybe the orientation of the can was wrong. It was currently wide from his perspective. He thought that maybe it should be long. Not willing to give up, Milan stopped to think again. Therefore, he went to the garbage can and rotated it by ninety degrees.

In the mean time, Stef's practice was progressing

and I was enjoying it. However, Milan's dilemma before me was very intriguing. Will he ever hit the trash can? Will he give up after a few attempts? Will he conclude that it was impossible? What other adjustments would he come up with? How long would it take?

Now that the can was positioned to give him a longer target to hit, he took a few shots to test his new theory. Hum. It does not seem to make a difference. He concluded that whether the can was positioned wide or long, it seemed that the angle played the biggest role in this puzzle.

After some thought, he turned the can to give him a wider target and proceeded to take a few shots to improve his choice of angle. All of a sudden he started to hit the rim. Hum... I thought that perhaps all those shots have improved his rubber band shooting skills after all.

Nope. It was just wishful thinking on my part. The band kept bouncing. Milan kept adjusting. And when he was just about ready to give up, the "swoosh" to end all "swooshing", he hit his desired target. He leaped to his feet with hands in the air in a Rocky like motion. "Yes! Yes! I did it...." And without a moment of hesitation, he looked at me and said, "Let's go Dad."

So what is a Dad to do? Milan did exactly what I wanted him to do. He made repeated attempts, strategic adjustments, experienced undesirable results, and at last achieved success. I had only but one choice. Leave the gym and go to the playground.

On the way out of the gym we passed an ice cream machine. Although ice cream was not a part of the deal, I threw in a sweetener so that the little guy felt rewarded. I was living up to the deal. Why not reward him for his effort?

However, it felt like something was missing. I had just spent the last 15-20 minutes watching my son achieve a goal. It was a difficult goal which required the use of patience, persistence, and effort to attain. The goal required strategy and repeated adjustments. His ultimate success required repeated failed attempts until he got the result that he wanted.

"Hummmmm....", I thought to myself. What a teachable moment.

I do not know if Milan understood what he did. Did he make the trash can by blind luck? Even if blind luck was involved, surely he can appreciate the effort that it took? His lack of excitement and ice cream dripping from the corner of his mouth led me to believe that maybe he had missed something.

As we walked towards the playground (about 200-300 feet away), I asked Milan a series of questions.

"Milan, did you hit the trash can on your first shot?"

"No way Dad!", said he.

"What happened then?"

"I believe I hit it short. It landed about a foot in front of the can. "

"Was that the result that you wanted? "

"No."

"So you did what?"

"I changed the angle. "

"Oh, you made an adjustment."

"How did that work out?"

"Not much better. I overshot the can."

"So you did not get the result you wanted?"

"No. "

"What did you do next?

"Well, I started thinking that the angle I was using was wrong and changed it a little bit."

"And that led to you hitting your target?"

"C'mon Dad, don't be silly. I missed it by a mile."

"No... you got a result that was not what you wanted."

"Yes."

"I then saw you change the way the can was facing."

"Yes, I did. I thought that since I had overshot by a little bit that if the can was placed the other way I would have a better chance of hitting it."

"Hum.."

"It did not work. I started using too much force and overshot the basket every time."

"So you put the basket back to its original position?"

Smack... lick.... bite.... Lick... smack... He was enjoying the ice cream.

"Yes."

"So what was happening?"

"Well, I kept making shots, missing my target, and then making changes in my strategy."

"What is another word for a target?"

"I do not know."

"How about a result? You wanted to hit the can. It was the result that you wanted."

"If you say so Dad."

I started to feel that Milan was getting tired of my million questions so I had to speed it up a bit.

While you were at the gym you took a bunch of shots. You tried to hit a target. Another word for a target is a result. You did not get the result that you wanted and after some thinking had to make a change. Let us call this change an adjustment. After you made the adjustments you got different results. Some were closer to your goal and some were not.

"Right?"

"Yes, that's what happened."

So after making many adjustments you finally got the result that you wanted.

"Can you repeat what I just told you?"

"I was trying to hit a rubber band inside a garbage can. I kept taking shots, missing the can, making small adjustments, and at last I got the result that I wanted."

"THAT IS IT!", I yelled out.

Notice that in your description you never used the word failure. There is no such thing. No matter what you are doing you will always get a result. It might not be the result that you want, so you have to make intelligent changes to your strategy, to get closer to your desired result. The key is in the intelligent changes. Just trying something different will get you a different result. But making intelligent changes will get you closer to your desired result a lot faster.

By this time we were approaching the playground and Milan requested that we play Mike Myers. I guess this is a game in which one pretends to be a killer slowly chasing a child around the playground. The child gets to scream at the top of their voice while running away until being caught.

As we proceeded with the chase, I crawled through tight places, climbed up steps, slid down a ramp, and continuously mumbled under my breath. Eventually I caught Milan who let out a laugh. We were enjoying our time together.

I told him I was proud of him and that I loved him. He said that he loved me too. I also told him that what he had learned is a very important lesson.

After some more playing around I was getting tired. Milan who at nine had played football with eleven year-olds seemed to have an overabundance of energy. He wanted to go again and continue the chase. I was getting tired and had to slow the pace. I had a better idea. I saw a set of monkey bars. It was an unusual set of monkey bars. They were positioned in a circle. Hum. When he was seven, I had seen Milan go down a couple of monkey bars and he never seemed to be able to get very far. So I offered a wager.

"Milan, if you can go all the way around the monkey bars I will give you a $10 bill", I said.

He said, "Are you sure?"

I said, "Yes."

The father in me wanted to test the new found knowledge that Milan had acquired. I expected him to get on the monkey bars, to get through a few bars, to fall down, and to get up. He would then walk up the steps to get to my level and then try again. Perhaps he would make an adjustment or two by twisting his body or even leaping forward to a bar up ahead?

I could not predict what he would do or what he was thinking, but I thought for sure that my bet was sound. There was no way a ten year old could go all the way around. He would try and try but eventually his arms would be tired and he would give up. He would then try to get me to break down and give him the $10 based on the effort alone and not on the final result.

I decided to make the wager very clear. I told him, "You can try as many times as you wish. You have to go all the way around and return to the platform after you have gone through the bars. You do not have to do one bar at a time but you can not touch the ground at all."

"Are you clear on this?"

"Yes."

"I will not pay if you do not reach the end.

Do you understand?"

"Yes I do."

"Ok, here I go", he said.

He leapt forward and twisted his body from one side to the other, holding on tightly, until he reached the final bar, and he leapt back on the platform.

A look of pride as well as shock was on my face.

"WOW, you did it."

"You did it...", I exclaimed.

"Yes I did!"

"What a difference between the rubber band and

the monkey bars?"

"Yes there was."

"So, what did you learn?"

"Well, I did not have to make many adjustments to reach the result that I wanted. I twisted and twisted and never let go of the bars. I did it!"

I gave him a hug and told him that that was exactly what I wanted him to say. I also pointed out that in the future he will never know how many adjustments it will take to get the result that he wants. In the monkey bar case he reached his goal in a single try.

The secret was to make intelligent adjustments until he got the result that he wanted. I explained to him that he should never look at results as failure. I said, "Totally replace the word failure from your vocabulary. Always think in terms of a result. What result did you get and what intelligent adjustments do you need to make, to get the result that you want to achieve."

He shook his head in agreement and we decided to get back to the gym to see the rest of Stef's practice. I figured that he was agreeable because it was an opportunity to brag about the money he had won. As we walked back to the gym, I lightly rubbed the top of his head to show my approval of him.

After the Practice

As we walked into the gym, the team was getting ready to call it a day. Milan was beaming from ear to ear. We sat on the bench and this time he patiently waited for his big sister.

The coaches finally called the practice to an end and told the kids to drink some water to rehydrate. They told the kids that they had worked hard and that they need to get ready for the game tomorrow at 1 p.m.

As Stefani approached the bench she could tell that Milan was unusually happy.

"What are you smiling about?"

"I got Dad for $10 bucks," he replied.

"How?"

"While you were practicing your game, Dad and I played a couple of games. The first game was a rubber band game. He had me shoot a rubber band at that garbage can over there from here."

"And you hit it?"

"Well, it was not easy. It took many adjustments to get the result that I wanted. "

"But, YES I hit it."

"So that is what you are all happy about?"

"You got $10 for hitting a garbage can with a rubber band?"

"No", he said.

"After I hit the trash can Dad bought me an ice cream and we went to the playground. As we walked we talked about the strategy and changes I used to get the result I wanted."

"I could do that", she boasted.

Milan laughed. "Yeah.. you think you can."

"I know I can." Stefani said with certainty.

Milan walked over to the garbage can and picked up the rubber band which was resting on top of some papers.

"Show me."

Stefani took the band and proceeded to make adjustments for a few minutes. Being a natural athlete, a bright seventh grader, and making the changes quickly, allowed her to hit the trash can a bit quicker.

"See I told you so."

"But that is not why I won $10 dollars. I went on the monkey bars all the way around the circle."

"Wow, that is pretty tough." Stefani acknowledged.

Watching the two of them discussing the events gave me an idea.

"Stefani, could you use what Milan said to improve your free throws?"

"Hum...I guess I could."

"I could shoot a free throw and watch the result. I would then make adjustments to improve my stroke."

"Ok Stefani, do it.", I said.

Stefani approached the free throw line, shot a basket, and missed.

"Ok, so what happened?"

"The shot barely hit the front of the rim."

"So what is the adjustment that you need to make?"

"I need to throw my shot a little harder."

"Try it."

She lobbed the ball toward the basket and the shot was a bit stronger. However this time the ball bounced off the backboard and hit the front of the rim on the way down.

"Ok, so what happened?"

"The shot was a little too hard and it bounced off the rim on its way down."

"So what is the adjustment that you need to make?"

"I need to throw my shot a little harder but with more of an arc."

"Try it", I said.

She shot the ball toward the basket a little harder and with an arc. The ball hit the area between the rim and the board and flew back with a lot of force.

"I don't think it is working Dad."

"You are getting better believe it or not. From the side it looked like it should have gone in. What adjustment can you make now?"

"Well, if I just hit the board a few inches above the rim it will bounce in the basket."

"Try it."

The ball went up and hit the spot a few inches above the rim, to the left, and on its way down hit the right side of the rim. Stefani sighed.

"Dad I noticed that most of the time I hit the rim on the left side."

"Yes."

"Why?"

"Well, notice that your feet are straight on the free throw line."

"Yes."

"Since you are a right hander, where does your right shoulder end up after your shot?"

"As I shoot, I twist my waist, and my shoulder ends up in the middle of my body."

"Well, that causes a curve to your shot and the ball goes towards the left side of the rim."

"So where should your right shoulder end up in

order for your shot to go straight?"

"It should end up straight with my left shoulder."

"Good observation."

"Try it."

She kept her feet together and shot a ball which hit the middle of the backboard box and it bounced in.

"Good."

"It seems that you have put all of the pieces together. Now try it again. Take 10 shots and let's see what happens."

Stefani stood at the line and took ten shots. She managed to get six out of the ten perfectly. The other four bounced off the left side of the rim.

"Hum."

"It seems that you are forcing your right shoulder to stop and not move past the left one."

After a little pause, I offered the following advice.

"What if you move your right foot back a few inches so that when you shoot the ball your right shoulder would naturally stop even with the left one?"

"Ok Dad, let me try another ten shots."

Stefani stepped up to the line and bounced the ball a few times and moved her right foot back about six inches. She took ten shots and managed to hit 80% of her shots.

"Great job!"

"Yes!"

"Is there anything else we can adjust?"

"I do not know Dad."

"How about slowing down?"

"What do you mean?"

"I think you need a routine. It seems to me that you need to slow down a bit. Bounce the ball a few times to get a feel for it, and then move your right foot back and spin the ball in your hands. Bounce the ball one time, look up at the basket, and shoot the ball at the top of the white box."

"I get it."

"You are trying to get me to focus on the ball instead of worrying about hitting the shot."

"Yes, that is a part of it."

"When you have a routine, it is easy to see which part of it is not working for you. If you notice that the shot is still hitting on the left side of the rim, then you need to move your right foot back a little more."

"Ok. I think I get it. I just have to practice my routine."

"Do you think you can improve the way your teammates shoot their free throws?"

"Well, I am the captain and they do listen to me."

"So, how will you gently share with them your new knowledge?"

"I think I need to demonstrate it to them."

"Once they see that I can hit 80% or more then they will pay attention."

"Maybe I need to tell them 'The Rubber Band Story'?"

We all laughed as we packed up and left the gym. We decided to head on back to their house. Milan sat in the back playing his PSP, and I drove, while Stefani bubbled about her newfound free-throw technique. She could not wait to share it with the team during their next practice.

When we arrived at their house, I got out of the car to say our goodbyes. I hugged and kissed them on their foreheads while telling them that I was proud of them. I told them that it was important to stay teachable as they were today.

They went inside the house and I headed back to the car. I sat inside the car for a moment, and remembered that I had forgotten something. I went back to the front door and knocked on it.

Milan came to the door and I smiled at him.

"I forgot something."

"What?"

"The $10 dollar bet."

"Oh."

I reached inside my pocket and handed him a crisp ten dollar bill.

He smiled and said, "Thanks. I think the lesson was worth a lot more."

"I agree."

"Enjoy your evening."

"You too."

"Love you."

"Love you too."

The following day at the game Stefani played quite well and scored 90% of her attempts from the free throw line.

Applications of the Story

To Parenthood

Our earliest exposure to the rubber band phenomenon occurs when we are babies. It has been so long ago that we have forgotten the lesson.

Imagine for a second that you are a parent of a baby who is about to walk. Your child stands up straight next to a table or a sofa. The baby tries to take a step and falls down. You smile to show your approval.

"Good job. Try again."

You help the baby up and move out of the way. The baby hesitates for a moment, but seeing your smile encourages it to try again.

This process continues for a while. Sometimes it takes days or weeks, BUT the attempt is always followed by a smile and encouraging words.

Interestingly, never during the process do you tell the baby to stop. Never are words of discouragement spoken. You expect the baby to eventually reach its goal of walking.

Now imagine if someone told you to tell the baby to stop trying. You would be offended. You might even become violent!

"How dare you say that? My baby will continue trying until he or she walks."

Again, the magic formula is to keep trying, with intelligent changes, until we get the result that we want. The story itself tells the application specifically to young children learning a valuable lesson.

Parenthood offers many opportunities for teaching children. At times, it is hard to find the "right" strategy for teaching your own kids lessons that will be valuable to them.

I find that while driving a car, I have a captive audience and it is a wonderful time to tell stories. Often, I take a story from a book I am reading and re-tell it to my kids at their level.

The question is, "How well does this work?" My kids are now 12 and 15 and I am amazed at how well they remember. Even when a long period of time has passed, sometimes years, and I start re-telling a story, sign of middle age, often times they interrupt me, to tell me that I have told them that story already and they know how it ends. Even at times when I felt that they might not have been paying attention, they were listening.

As an unexpected benefit, I often find that telling business or self-help stores helps to teach them new vocabulary words. They normally would not come across these stories and words in their classes. This is a win-win for everyone.

My advice is to see the whole parenting process as the rubber band story. You make an attempt, make intelligent adjustments, and eventually get the result that you want.

To School

What happens when a child comes home with a report card from school with five As and one B? A parent looks at the B and starts to ask questions.

"Why did you get a B in subject XYZ?"

"I don't know."

"Come on, you know."

"I don't know, the teacher just does not like me."

Usually the answer does not offer any room for improvement. The mistaken goal is to have a perfect report card with all As.

The As are an extrinsic goal. It is one that the child and you can boast about. However, that is not the true goal of going to school.

The true motivation for school achievement should be intrinsic. Is the child developing techniques and strategies for how to learn? If the child can be given strategies on how to learn then the process of learning becomes a joyful experience.

How does one convert this extrinsic goal into an intrinsic goal? For most of our early life we were endowed with intrinsic curiosity. That is why we ask why so many times until we finally get it. Therefore, we have to nurture the process instead of focusing only on the ultimate goal.

Using the rubber band story, one can see that we need to focus on the result but also offer meaningful adjustments to help the child to succeed extrinsically. What about intrinsically? This too can be achieved by noting that we need to praise the natural built-in curiosity that kids are born with when they enter into this world.

One way of helping children nurture their curiosity is to become more curious yourself. As a matter of fact, show an interest in their work, have them teach you what they know. You will quickly see how to expand the level of their current curiosity (current result) and to offer a meaningful adjustment to drive them towards increased curiosity (the desired result).

I have found that even with my college math students this technique works. Often times my students are assigned to work on a specific set of problems using software called Aleks. I sell them on Aleks by telling them that Aleks is their best friend. Aleks will offer a problem and they will attempt to solve it. If they do not understand it or get it wrong, Aleks will give them an explanation on how to solve the problem. Then being their best friend it will generate a similar problem for them to solve. Wow! It is the rubber band story built into the software. The desired result for each problem is to learn how to solve one particular type of problem.

Students, because they are forced to spend hours and hours with Aleks, tend to dislike the program because it does not offer partial credit. The answer is either correct or not. Aleks gives them an honest assessment of their result.

This is something with which we as parents and teachers often struggle. However, honest feedback and helpful adjustments will help them to obtain the desired result.

To Business

Quick. What was Sony's first product that the company ever produced? If you answered a rice cooker then move to the front of the line.

What? A rice cooker! Yes. So how does a company go from building rice cookers to the electronic giant that it is today? Think about the rubber band story.

The company obtained a result with its rice cooker. It was considered a failure. It was probably not the result that they wanted. So they made an adjustment after an adjustment until it was what they wanted. Somewhere along the way they changed their goal to electronics.

Consider Tiger Woods for a moment. A few years ago he was at the top of his game when he decided to completely change his swing. He realized that even though he was getting very good results and green jackets that he was not at his best. In order to get the results that he wanted, he scrapped everything and hired a coach to completely change his swing. I am sure that he had to make many small intelligent changes to get the result that he was trying to achieve.

Interesting? What do most start-up companies do? They put out a product and observe the results. Once the results and comments come in, they produce a version 2.0. This gives them a product and a result closer to their desired result.

Consider what would happen if a company did not release the version 1.0 and instead went for version Perfect Product version 1.0? They might get lucky by completely understanding what their customer wants. But while the company was perfecting it, the product did not earn any revenue as well as valuable input from the customers on how to make the product better.

Which way would you or your company be better off?

To Teams

I often teach Business and MBA courses. In these courses students tend to work on group projects. The team dynamics are not always helpful for the team to achieve their best work.

On each team there tends to be at least one person who wants to be the leader. The leader is most often focused on the task and not the group's feelings. Often there are other team members that tend to want to talk only about their feelings and focus less on the task. Some members might desire to be everyone's best friend and do not want any conflict. Lastly, there might be a perfectionist, or two, that refuses to do sub-standard work.

Is it any wonder why team work is often the most painful part of any project? Does it have to be that way? No. I often allow the students to go through a few weeks of meeting with each other, before I administer a personality test that scores them along these four dimensions: leadership, communication, friendliness, and perfectionism. Once the individual scores are placed on the board for each team, I review the dynamics of the teams. At this point, I see a lot of mouths drop in disbelief of how accurately I can describe meetings at which I was not present.

At this point they have gotten some results and have observed the group dynamics, I offer individual adjustments that each person can contribute to make the team more effective. I then ask them to model these new behaviors for the rest of the semester. The final result is often orders of magnitude better than allowing the team dynamics to just play out.

Ask yourself: how well can you describe your team members', your spouse's, or your child's personalities? The test that I use was developed by Gary Smiley. I first read about this test in a book by Steven A. Scott called <u>Mentored by a Millionaire</u>.

Many organizations use the DISC (Drive, Influence, Steadiness, and Compliance) profile to evaluate their employees' personality. However, they never extract that individual information to teams. This is where the full benefit of the personality tests could be obtained.

Note: This topic is covered in my upcoming "I Hate You... I Really Hate YOU! How to Build a Functional Team When Everyone is Dysfunctional" book.

To Investing

Another one of my many projects is an ETFs (Exchange Traded Funds) Book for Non-Dummies. In the book I teach how to pick the best ETF funds that match the investor's criteria while developing your own system.

Many times I teach the techniques from the book in my business and MBA courses. After having the students learn how to pick the funds that best fit their investment profile, we go through a five-week competition to see who makes the most money. They initially choose up to five funds to invest in using paper money.

Often the fund choices that the student makes initially have

problems and the students are forced to make adjustments and choose new ones. The new choices are still based on their investment profile but contain information that is more current. This allows them to continue playing the game while trying to achieve the goal of getting the best return.

The secret to this project is to keep track of their investments and to report their current financial status every week. In a sense, I am trying to teach them how to apply the rubber band story to develop their own system.

Quite often the students understand my system but choose to make their own decisions based on gut feelings. This often leads to a reduction in performance.

The moral of the story is to have a system in place by which you make intelligent changes to your strategy. If your change is solely based on a guess or a hunch then it most likely will not result in the gains that you hope.

To Self-Improvement

Can the rubber band story be applied to the individual? Well, the story is all about the individual. It was my son's quest to reach his goal of hitting the rubber band inside the trash can. It was also about my daughter's journey to becoming a better free-throw shooter and improving her teammates.

From a self-help perspective, life is full of results in many different areas of life. Every day we get results. The unfortunate part is that we do not sit down long enough in our crazy busy life, to pause and evaluate these results.

My recommendation is to sit quietly at the end of each day and review the results that you obtained that day. Using a piece a paper and pen jot down the different results. Ask yourself if those results were the ones you wanted. If they were not, then spend some time considering a meaningful and intelligent change you can make in each area, to get you closer to the desired result. Now the hard part, put it on your "to do" list for tomorrow or next time you are scheduled to do this activity. The magic is to stay conscious and to use the modification and review the result.

In a sense, the rubber band story is no different than the Bill Murray's Groundhog Day movie. In the movie, a weather man finds himself living the same day over and over again.

Every day we are involved in many situations that tend to repeat themselves. Can we make intelligent changes to our actions that will get us closer to a more desirable result?

Yes!

CAUTION: Self-improvement should not be looked at as an achievable goal. Dan Sullivan in his book Pure Genius offers an analogy of self-improvement to a horizon. No matter how hard we can try to reach the horizon, we are not upset that we do not reach the horizon. It is the search towards that goal that makes the journey worthwhile.

I once heard a story of someone approaching Zig Ziglar and telling him that he got a lot of out the seminar. The person proceeded to say that unfortunately the effect of the seminar is only short lived. Zig replied "So is bathing. That is why we have to do it everyday."

To Writing a Book

Can the rubber band story be applied to writing a book? I can tell you with certainty that it was applied to this book. After the initial idea was obvious and I felt the need to create it, I wrote a brief outline on my cell phone while at a basketball game.

Next I took the outline and over a week I added additional details to each bullet. I kept doing this until I felt that each point, indicated with a bullet, and sub-bullets would produce a page in the book. I continued making adjustments to the order until I was satisfied with complete outline.

The writing process was quite straight forward. I had the outline in front of me so I could just focus on the writing. This helped me to be able to quickly write the book.

I then approached my kids to read the book and get their reaction. The smiles on their faces about being characters in a book gave me the energy to make several editing changes.

Now that I was pleased with my intermediate result, I let ten co-workers and friends read the book. Their feedback was very important and I quickly learned of some obvious mistakes that I had made. I also learned that most people are not very good editors. They will provide you with insight into the quality of the product but not necessarily catch actual mistakes.

Luckily, a few were very good and provided good editorial insight. However, I had to be cautious. The danger of outright following their advice might lead to completely changing the book that I wrote. I wanted the book flow to be as if a friend were telling you a story and NOT very preachy.

Well, after numerous results I thought I was done and gave the book to two last co-workers to read. I expected them to come back indicating to me that I had reached my goal. However, this did not happen.

One offered a few word changes and another offered that I should add a section on how I applied this idea to writing this book.

Hum... Back to the drawing board I went and did as they suggested.

I was close to the goal but still made these changes. However, I decided that they would be the final readers. I felt that I had reached my goal and that I was now ready to give my book a nudge out of the nest.

SUMMARY

Just remember. In everything:

1. Identify the goal you want to reach

2. Make an initial attempt towards it

3. Observe the result that you have obtained

4. Pause to think. THIS IS CRITICAL!

5. Brainstorm different actions that will bring you closer to the desired result.

6. Consciously make a single change that you believe will bring you closer to the desired result.

7. If you do not get the desired result, go back to step 3

8. Have fun... the journey is the magic...

Why the Infinite Rubber Band on the Front Cover and Multiple Rubber Bands on the Back?

While learning math a student is exposed to the concept of infinity. It illustrates a concept without a bound. The symbol that is assigned to this concept by mathematicians is: ∞. (See the front cover image)

I chose the symbol and created the covers to illustrate that the story has infinite possibilities for improvement. As I illustrated in the brief application section, the concept can be used to improve the results that you achieve in all areas of life.

It is a journey on which you consciously take note of the results and make what seems like numerous, and at times infinite changes, until you get the result that you want.

A single rubber band on the front cover signifies that, like my son, it might take only one attempt to achieve your goal. In reality, the number of attempts will vary with the task that is being solved. The multiple color rubber bands on the back indicate that often times it requires multiple attempts to achieve the desired goal.

So remember...

Enjoy the journey, make many intelligent adjustments, and once in a while look up towards the final result that you desire. It will result in a life changing process.

Robert Trajkovski

12/6/2010